sinful
chocolate

Published by:
TRIDENT REFERENCE PUBLISHING
801 12th Avenue South, Suite 400
Naples, Fl 34102 USA

Tel: + 1 (239) 649-7077
www.tridentreference.com
email: sales@tridentreference.com

sinful chocolate

Sinful Chocolate
© TRIDENT REFERENCE PUBLISHING

Publisher
Simon St. John Bailey

Editor-in-chief
Susan Knightley

Prepress
Precision Prep & Press

Includes Index
ISBN 1582797250
UPC 6 15269 97250 2

Printed in The United States

introduction

Whatever the occasion, chocolate is a celebration all of its own. This collection of mouthwatering cakes, creamy puddings, luscious desserts and tempting sweet bites is guaranteed to gladden the hearts and delight the taste buds of chocolate lovers. Whether you yearn for old favorites, chocolatey home bakes or a spectacular centerpiece for a special

celebration, these recipes are sure to satisfy the longings of even the most discerning chocoholics. Before trying them, give a glance to the following watch points.

Storing Chocolate

Chocolate should be stored in a dry, airy place at a temperature of about 16°C/60° F. If stored in unsuitable conditions, the cocoa butter in chocolate may rise to the surface, leaving a white film. A similar discoloration occurs when water condenses on the surface. This often happens to refrigerated chocolates that are too loosely wrapped. Chocolate affected this way is still suitable for melting, but not for grating.

Melting Chocolate

- Chocolate melts more rapidly if broken into small pieces.

- The melting process should occur slowly. Do not melt chocolate over a direct flame.

- To melt chocolate, place it in a heatproof bowl set over a saucepan of simmering water, taking care the water does not touch the bottom of the bowl. Stir occasionally until the chocolate melts and is of a smooth consistency. Cool at room temperature.

- Keep the container in which the chocolate is being melted, uncovered and completely dry. Covering could cause condensation and just one drop of water will ruin the chocolate.

- Chocolate "seizes" if it is overheated or if it comes in contact with water or steam. Seizing results in the chocolate tightening and becoming a thick mass that will not melt.

- To rescue seized chocolate, stir in a little cream or vegetable oil until the chocolate becomes smooth again.

- Chocolate can be melted quickly and easily in the microwave. Cook on High (100%) for 2 minutes per 400 g chocolate, stir. If chocolate is not completely melted, cook it for an extra 20-30 seconds, then stir again.

Difficulty scale

■ □ □ I Easy to do

■ ■ □ I Requires attention

■ ■ ■ I Requires experience

sacher torte

a

■□□ I Cooking time: 25 minutes - Preparation time: 15 minutes

method

1. Place butter, sugar and vanilla essence in a bowl and beat until light and fluffy. Gradually beat in eggs.

2. Sift together flour, cocoa powder and baking powder over butter mixture (a). Add buttermilk and mix well to combine.

3. Pour mixture into two greased and lined 23 cm/9 in cake tins and bake at 180°C/350°F/Gas 4 for 25 minutes or until cakes are cooked when tested with a skewer. Stand cakes in tins for 5 minutes before turning onto wire racks to cool.

4. To make glaze, place chocolate and butter in a heatproof bowl set over a saucepan of simmering water and heat, stirring, until mixture is smooth. Remove bowl from pan and set aside to cool until mixture thickens and is of a spreadable consistency.

5. To assemble cake, place one cake on a serving plate and spread with jam (b). Top with remaining cake and spread top and sides with glaze (c).

Serves 8-10

ingredients

> **250 g/8 oz butter,** softened
> **1 1/2 cups/265 g/8 1/2 oz** brown sugar
> **2 teaspoons vanilla** essence
> **2 eggs, lightly beaten**
> **1 1/2 cups/185 g/6 oz** flour
> **2/3 cup/60 g/2 oz cocoa** powder
> **3/4 teaspoon baking** powder
> **1 1/2 cups/375 ml/** 12 fl oz buttermilk
> **1/2 cup/155 g/5 oz** apricot jam

dark chocolate glaze

> **185 g/6 oz dark** chocolate, broken into pieces
> **185 g/6 oz butter,** chopped

tip from the chef

This Austrian favorite comes complete with a hidden layer of apricot jam. The words "Sacher Torte" piped onto the top of the cake in chocolate adds a touch of authenticity to the decoration.

b

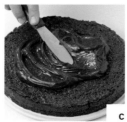

c

white
chocolate yogurt cake

■□□ | Cooking time: 50 minutes - Preparation time: 15 minutes

ingredients

> **155 g/5 oz white chocolate, broken into pieces**
> **2 cups/250 g/8 oz self-raising flour**
> **1 cup/220 g/7 oz caster sugar**
> **2 eggs, lightly beaten**
> **200 g/6^1/$_2$ oz natural yogurt**
> **45 g/1^1/$_2$ oz butter, melted**

white chocolate glaze

> **75 g/2^1/$_2$ oz white chocolate**
> **1 tablespoon double cream**

method

1. Place chocolate in a heatproof bowl set over a saucepan of simmering water and heat, stirring, until smooth. Remove bowl from pan and cool slightly.
2. Place flour, sugar, eggs, yogurt and butter in a bowl and beat for 5 minutes or until mixture is smooth. Add melted chocolate and mix well to combine.
3. Pour mixture into a greased 23 cm/9 in ring tin and bake at 180°C/350°F/Gas 4 for 50 minutes or until cake is cooked when tested with a skewer. Stand cake in tin for 5 minutes before turning onto a wire rack to cool.
4. To make glaze, place chocolate and cream in a heatproof bowl set over a saucepan of simmering water and heat, stirring, until mixture is smooth. Spread glaze over top and sides of cake.

Makes a 23 cm/9 in ring cake

tip from the chef

Once glaze is set, decorate with white chocolate shavings (page 60).

rich
devil's food cake

■□□ | Cooking time: 45 minutes - Preparation time: 15 minutes

method

1. Place butter and caster sugar in a bowl and beat until light and fluffy. Gradually beat in eggs.
2. Sift together flour, cocoa powder and baking powder over butter mixture. Add milk and food coloring and mix well to combine.
3. Pour mixture into two greased and lined 20 cm/8 in round cake tins and bake at 180°C/350°F/Gas 4 for 45 minutes or until cakes are cooked when tested with a skewer. Stand cakes in tins for 5 minutes before turning onto wire racks to cool.
4. To make filling, place cream in a bowl and beat until soft peaks form. Fold in chocolate.
5. To assemble cake, place one cake on a serving plate. Spread with jam and filling and top with remaining cake. Just prior to serving, dust top of cake with icing sugar. From greaseproof paper, cut a template of a devil's fork. Lay template on top of cake and dust with cocoa powder.

ingredients

> 185 g/6 oz butter, softened
> 1³/₄ cups/375 g/12 oz caster sugar
> 3 eggs
> 2 cups/250 g/8 oz flour
> ²/₃ cup/60 g/2 oz cocoa powder
> 1¹/₂ teaspoons baking powder
> 1 cup/250 ml/8 fl oz milk
> few drops red food coloring
> ¹/₂ cup/155 g/5 oz raspberry jam
> icing sugar and extra cocoa powder, sifted, for decorating

chocolate cream filling

> ¹/₂ cup/125 ml/4 fl oz double cream
> 90 g/3 oz dark chocolate, melted and cooled

....
Serves 8

tip from the chef

It's the red food coloring that gives this cake its devilishly deep mahogany hue.

chocolate gold

■□□ I Cooking time: 30 minutes - Preparation time: 15 minutes

ingredients

chocolate cake

> **250 g/8 oz dark chocolate, broken into pieces**
> **155 g/5 oz butter, chopped**
> **4 eggs, separated**
> **3/4 cup/185 g/6 oz sugar**
> **1/3 cup/45 g/1 1/2 oz flour, sifted**
> **gold leaf**

chocolate mirror glaze

> **250 g/8 oz dark chocolate, broken into pieces**
> **3 teaspoons vegetable oil**

method

1. To make cake, place chocolate and butter in a heatproof bowl set over a saucepan of simmering water and heat, stirring, until mixture is smooth. Remove bowl from pan and set aside to cool.
2. Place egg yolks and sugar in a bowl and beat until thick and pale. Fold flour and chocolate mixture into egg yolk mixture. Place egg whites in a clean bowl and beat until stiff peaks form. Fold egg whites into chocolate mixture.
3. Pour mixture into a greased and lined 23 cm/9 in springform tin and bake at 160°C/325°F/Gas 3 for 30 minutes or until cake is cooked when tested with a skewer. Cool cake in tin.
4. To make glaze, place chocolate in a heatproof bowl set over a saucepan of simmering water and heat, stirring, until chocolate melts and is smooth. Stir in oil and mix until combined.
5. Remove cake from tin and place on a wire rack. Pour glaze over cake and allow it to run over sides. Allow to set. Decorate with gold leaf and serve with cream.

....
Serves 12

tip from the chef

The bottom of a baked cake is often smoother than the top so to ensure a perfectly smooth surface for glazing, invert the cooled cake onto another springform base or a 23 cm/9 in circle of foil-covered cardboard.

chocolate
espresso cheesecake

a

b

c

■□□ I Cooking time: 40 minutes - Preparation time: 15 minutes

method

1. To make base, place biscuit crumbs and butter in a bowl and mix to combine. Press mixture (a) over the base of a lightly greased and lined 20 cm/8 in springform tin. Refrigerate until firm.
2. To make filling, place coffee powder and water in a bowl and mix until coffee powder dissolves. Set aside to cool slightly.
3. Place cream cheese, sour cream, eggs, sugar and coffee mixture in a bowl (b) and beat until smooth.
4. Pour half the filling over prepared base. Drop 4 tablespoons of melted chocolate into filling and swirl with a skewer (c). Repeat with remaining filling and chocolate and bake at 200°C/400°F/Gas 6 for 40 minutes or until cheesecake is firm. Cool in tin.
5. To make glaze, place liqueur and rum into a saucepan and bring to simmering over a medium heat. Simmer, stirring occasionally, until mixture reduces to 1/4 cup/60 ml/2 fl oz. Add chocolate, butter and cream and cook, stirring, until mixture is smooth. Remove pan from heat and set aside until mixture thickens slightly. Spread glaze over cheesecake and allow to set.

ingredients

> 250 g/8 oz chocolate wafer biscuits, crushed
> 155 g/5 oz butter, melted

chocolate espresso filling

> 2 tablespoons instant espresso coffee powder
> 1 tablespoon hot water
> 250 g/8 oz cream cheese, softened
> 1 cup/250 g/8 oz sour cream
> 3 eggs, lightly beaten
> 1 cup/250 g/8 oz sugar
> 155 g/5 oz dark chocolate, melted

coffee liqueur glaze

> 1/4 cup/60 ml/2 fl oz coffee-flavored liqueur
> 1/4 cup/60 ml/2 fl oz rum
> 250 g/8 oz dark chocolate, broken into pieces
> 60 g/2 oz butter
> 1/2 cup/125 ml/4 fl oz double cream

Serves 10

tip from the chef

To prevent the cheesecake from cracking as it cools, bake until a knife inserted just off center comes out clean, then place cake in a draught-free place or in the turned-off oven with the door ajar until cooled completely.

hearts
of chocolate

■■□ I Cooking time: 40 minutes - Preparation time: 10 minutes

ingredients

> **125 g/4 oz butter, softened**
> **1 cup/250 g/8 oz sugar**
> **1 teaspoon vanilla essence**
> **2 eggs, lightly beaten**
> **1³/4 cups/155 g/5 oz self-raising flour**
> **¹/2 cup/45 g/1¹/2 oz cocoa powder**
> **1 teaspoon bicarbonate of soda**
> **1 cup/250 ml/8 fl oz milk**
> cocoa powder, sifted
> white and dark chocolate curls (page 60)

creamy chocolate filling

> **375 g/12 oz milk chocolate, broken into pieces**
> **155 g/5 oz butter, chopped**
> **³/4 cup/185 ml/6 fl oz double cream**

method

1. Place butter, sugar and vanilla essence in a bowl and beat until light and fluffy. Gradually beat in eggs.

2. Sift flour, cocoa powder and bicarbonate of soda together into a bowl. Fold flour mixture and milk alternately into egg mixture.

3. Pour mixture into a greased and base-lined heart-shaped cake tin and bake at 190°C/375°F/Gas 5 for 40 minutes or until cake is cooked when tested with a skewer. Stand cake in tin for 5 minutes. Turn onto a wire rack to cool.

4. Trim top of cake and turn cake upside down. Scoop out center of cake leaving a 2 cm/³/4 in border. Do not cut right the way through the cake, but leave 2 cm/³/4 in cake to form the base.

5. To make filling, place chocolate, butter and cream in a heatproof bowl set over a saucepan of simmering water and heat, stirring, until mixture is smooth. Remove bowl from pan and set aside to cool. Beat until light and creamy. Pour filling into prepared cake and chill for 4 hours or until filling is firm.

6. Place cake on a serving plate. Dust top with cocoa powder and decorate with chocolate curls.

tip from the chef

This basic butter cake is a good one for baking in muffin or patty tins for individual servings in school or office lunch boxes.

....
Serves 10

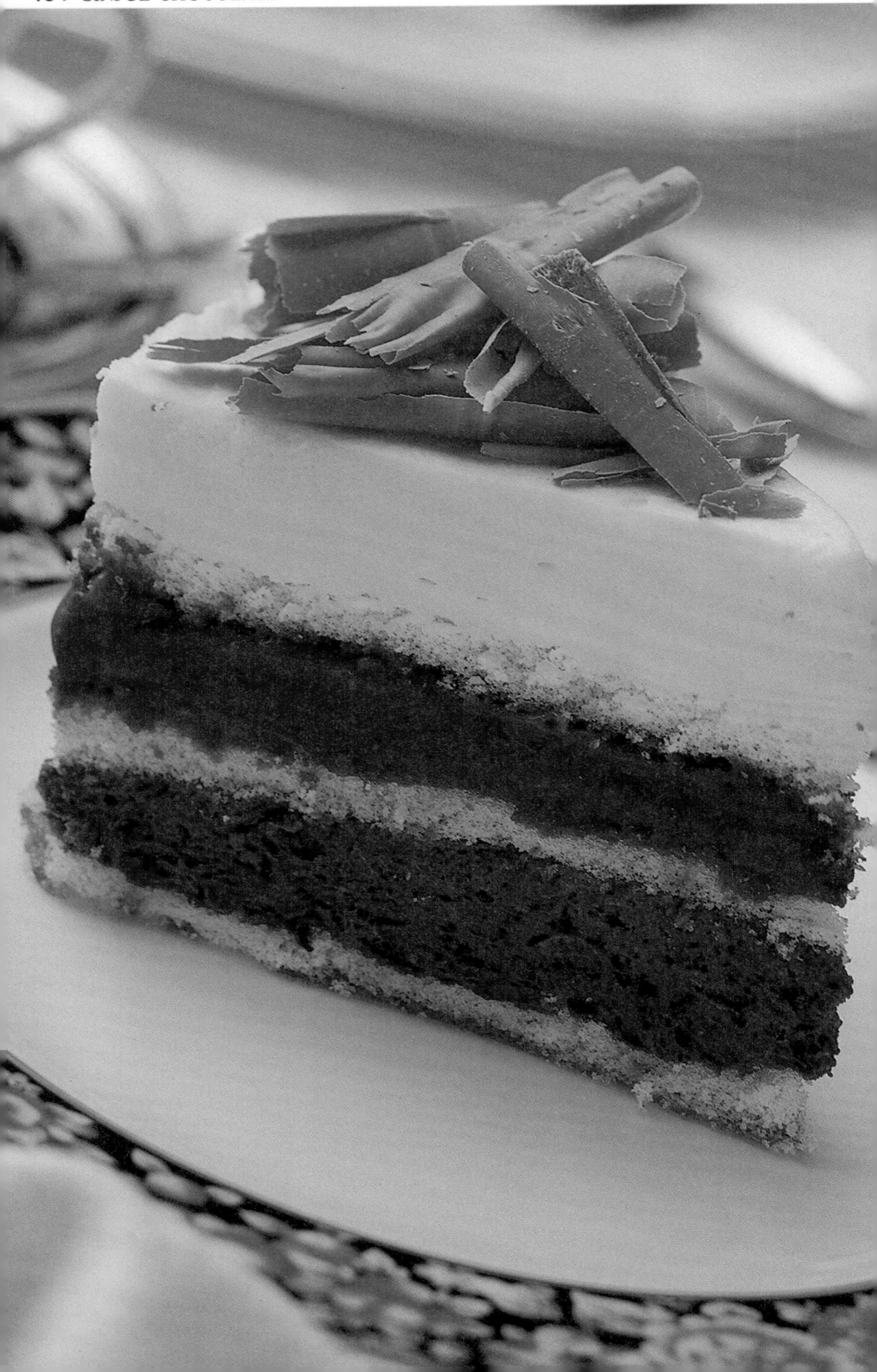

triple
mousse cake

■ ■ □ I Cooking time: 0 minute - Preparation time: 15 minutes

method

1. Cut sponge horizontally into three even layers and place one layer in base of a lined 23 cm/9 in springform tin.
2. To make dark mousse, mix chocolate, brandy and egg yolk. Beat egg whites in a clean bowl until soft peaks form. Gradually beat in sugar and continue beating until stiff peaks form. Fold chocolate mixture and cream into egg whites. Pour mousse over sponge and chill for 1 hour or until firm. Top with a second sponge layer.
3. To make mocha mousse, mix chocolate, coffee and egg yolk. Beat egg whites in a clean bowl until soft peaks form. Gradually beat in sugar and continue beating until stiff peaks form. Fold chocolate mixture and cream into egg whites. Pour mousse over sponge and chill for 1 hour or until firm. Top with remaining sponge layer.
4. To make white mousse, place chocolate and milk in a heatproof bowl set over a saucepan of simmering water and stir until smooth. Cool slightly. Fold chocolate mixture into cream. Pour mousse over sponge. Chill for 3 hours or until firm.

ingredients

> 1 x 23 cm/9 in sponge cake

dark mousse

> 185 g/6 oz dark chocolate, melted
> 2 tablespoons brandy
> 1 egg yolk
> 2 egg whites
> 1 tablespoon sugar
> $1/3$ cup/90 ml/3 fl oz double cream, whipped

mocha mousse

> 185 g/6 oz milk chocolate
> 2 tablespoons strong black coffee
> 1 egg yolk
> 2 egg whites
> 1 tablespoon sugar
> $1/3$ cup/90 ml/3 fl oz double cream, whipped

white mousse

> 185 g/6 oz white chocolate
> 2 tablespoons milk
> 1 cup/250 ml/8 fl oz double cream, whipped

Serves 12

tip from the chef

Serve this elegant chocoholic's delight with a sweetened purée of fresh sieved raspberries or strawberries.

chocolate
dessert cake

■ ■ □ | Cooking time: 35 minutes - Preparation time: 15 minutes

ingredients

> **6 eggs, separated**
> **1/2 cup caster sugar**
> **1/4 cup cocoa powder**
> **200 g/61/2 oz dark chocolate, melted**
> **icing sugar for dusting**
> **1 cup cream**
> **2 tablespoons brandy**
> **1/2 cup caster sugar, extra**

method

1. Beat egg yolks and sugar in a medium bowl with an electric mixer until creamy. Mix in cocoa powder and dark chocolate, mix well.
2. In a separate bowl, beat egg whites with electric mixer until soft peaks form. Fold egg whites into chocolate mixture until just combined.
3. Pour mixture into a greased and lined 23 cm/9 in springform pan and bake in a moderate oven for 35 minutes, allow cake to cool completely before removing from pan, dust with icing sugar.
4. Beat cream with brandy until slightly thickened, but still of pouring consistency. Refrigerate.
5. Melt sugar in a medium saucepan over high heat, moving saucepan around so sugar browns evenly. Bring to the boil, do not stir, cook until toffee is a light golden color. Pour toffee onto a sheet of lightly greased foil or greaseproof paper and set aside. When set break up toffee.
6. To serve, pour about 4 tablespoons of cream mixture onto each plate, place a slice of dessert cake on the cream and decorate with the broken toffee.

....
Serves 8

tip from the chef

Another tempting option is to serve this cake with a berry sauce.

checkerboard
cake

I☐I Cooking time: 30 minutes - Preparation time: 30 minutes

method

1. Sift together flour, baking powder and bicarbonate of soda in a bowl. Add sugar, butter and milk and beat until smooth. Divide mixture into two equal portions.
2. Combine white chocolate and 2 teaspoons oil and fold into one portion of mixture. Pour into a greased and lined 18 cm/7 in square cake tin.
3. Combine dark chocolate and remaining oil and fold into remaining portion of mixture. Pour into a second greased and lined 18 cm/7 in square cake tin.
4. Bake cakes at 180°C/350°F/Gas 4 for 30 minutes or until cooked when tested with a skewer. Stand cakes in tins for 5 minutes before turning onto wire racks to cool.
5. To make filling, place all ingredients in a heatproof bowl set over a saucepan of simmering water and heat, stirring, until mixture is smooth. Chill for 30 minutes or until filling thickens and is easy to spread.
6. To assemble cake, cut each cake into six even strips. Place a strip of white cake on a rack, spread one side with a little filling and press a strip of chocolate cake against it. Repeat to make a base of alternating colors. Spread top with filling. Then use another four strips of cake to make a second and a third layer so that colors alternate with those on the base. Spread remaining filling over top and sides of cake.

....
Serves 12

ingredients

> 2¹/2 cups/315 g/10 oz flour
> 1 teaspoon baking powder
> ³/4 teaspoon bicarbonate of soda
> 2 cups/440 g/14 oz caster sugar
> 250 g/8 oz butter, softened
> 1¹/2 cups/375 ml/ 12 fl oz buttermilk or milk
> 60 g/2 oz white chocolate, melted
> 4 teaspoons vegetable oil
> 60 g/2 oz dark chocolate, melted

chocolate filling

> 375 g/12 oz milk chocolate, broken into pieces
> 280 g/9 oz butter, chopped
> 1¹/2 tablespoons light golden syrup

tip from the chef

This pretty cake is well worth the effort and not difficult to assemble. Take your time when cutting the layers to achieve uniform pieces with straight, even edges.

chocolate
mousse cake

■■□ | Cooking time: 5 minutes - Preparation time: 20 minutes

method

1. To make filling, place chocolate and butter in a heatproof bowl set over a saucepan of simmering water and heat, stirring constantly, until mixture is smooth. Remove bowl from pan and set aside to cool slightly. Beat egg yolks into chocolate mixture and fold in cream.
2. Using a serrated edged knife, cut cake into three even layers. Brush each layer with brandy. Place one layer of cake in the base of a 23 cm/9 in lined springform tin. Spoon one-third of the filling over cake in tin. Top with a second layer of cake and half the remaining mousse. Repeat layers. Refrigerate for 4 hours or until firm. Unmold and decorate with chocolate caraques.

ingredients

> 1 x 23 cm/9 in chocolate sponge or butter cake
> 2 tablespoons brandy
> chocolate caraques (page 60) or chocolate sticks, for decoration

mousse filling

> 500 g/1 lb dark chocolate, chopped
> 125 g/4 oz butter
> 2 egg yolks
> 1¹/₂ cups/375 ml/ 12 fl oz double cream, whipped

....
Makes a 23 cm/9 in round cake

tip from the chef

The chocolate butter cake recipe on page 16 can be used for this recipe.

Line the springform tin base and sides with greaseproof paper for easier unmolding.

light
chocolate brownies

■□□ | Cooking time: 30 minutes - Preparation time: 5 minutes

method

1. Sift together flour, baking powder and cocoa powder into a bowl. Add sugar, yogurt, eggs, vanilla essence and oil and mix to combine.
2. Spoon batter into a 20 cm/8 in square nonstick tin and bake at 180°C/350°F/ Gas 4 for 25-30 minutes.
3. Allow brownies to cool in tin before turning out and cutting into squares.

....
Makes 16

ingredients

> ³/4 cup/90 g/3 oz flour
> ¹/2 teaspoon baking powder
> ¹/2 cup/45 g/1¹/2 oz cocoa powder
> 1 cup/ 220 g/7 oz caster sugar
> ¹/2 cup/100 g/3 oz vanilla yogurt
> 2 eggs
> 1 teaspoon vanilla essence
> 1¹/2 tablespoons vegetable oil

tip from the chef

If you do not have a nonstick tin, line tin with nonstick baking paper.

double
choc brownies

■□□ | Cooking time: 40 minutes - Preparation time: 5 minutes

method

1. Place sugar, chocolate, oil, vanilla essence and eggs in a bowl and whisk to combine. Sift together flour and baking powder. Add flour mixture to chocolate mixture (a) and mix well to combine.
2. Pour mixture into a greased and lined 20 cm/8 in square cake tin and bake at 180°C/350°F/Gas 4 for 40 minutes or until firm to touch.
3. Cool in tin, then cut into 5 cm/2 in squares (b) and place on a wire rack.
4. To make glaze, place chocolate in a heatproof bowl set over a saucepan of simmering water and heat, stirring, until chocolate melts. Stir in oil. Spoon glaze over brownies (c) and stand until set.

....
Makes 20

ingredients

> 1½ cups/375 g/12 oz sugar
> 200 g/6½ oz dark chocolate, melted
> 1 cup/250 ml/8 fl oz vegetable oil
> 2 teaspoons vanilla essence
> 4 eggs
> 1¾ cups/220 g/7 oz flour
> 1 teaspoon baking powder

chocolate glaze

> 185 g/6 oz dark chocolate
> 2 teaspoons vegetable oil

tip from the chef

These intensely chocolatey and tender treats will stay moist and delicious for several days if stored in an airtight container in a cool, dry place.

a

b

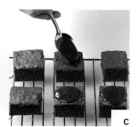

c

tiny fudge cakes

■□□ I Cooking time: 10 minutes - Preparation time: 15 minutes

method

1. Place dark chocolate and butter in a heatproof bowl set over a saucepan of simmering water and heat, stirring, until mixture is smooth. Remove bowl from pan and set aside to cool slightly.

2. Place egg yolks and sugar in a bowl and beat until thick and pale. Fold flour into egg mixture. Add chocolate mixture to egg mixture and mix to combine.

3. Place egg whites into a clean bowl and beat until stiff peaks form. Fold egg whites into chocolate mixture.

4. Spoon mixture into greased mini cup cake tins or small paper cup cake cases and bake at 180°C/350°F/Gas 4 for 10 minutes. Remove cakes from tins and cool on wire racks.

5. To make glaze, place white chocolate and cream in a heatproof bowl set over a saucepan of simmering water and heat, stirring, until mixture is smooth. Remove bowl from pan and set aside until mixture thickens slightly. Spread glaze over cakes and decorate with sugared violets.

ingredients

> **100 g/3¹/₂ oz dark chocolate**
> **60 g/2 oz butter**
> **3 eggs, separated**
> **¹/₂ cup/100 g/3¹/₂ oz caster sugar**
> **¹/₄ cup/30 g/1 oz flour, sifted**

white chocolate glaze

> **100 g/3¹/₂ oz white chocolate, chopped**
> **2 tablespoons double cream**
> **sugared violets**

....
Makes 20

tip from the chef

Sugared violets are available from cake decorators' suppliers and specialty kitchen shops.

chocolate
hazelnut puddings

■□□ | Cooking time: 10 minutes - Preparation time: 15 minutes

method

1. Prepare a six-hole microwavable muffin tray by brushing with melted butter and coating evenly with caster sugar. Place 1 teaspoon marmalade in each hole.
2. Melt chocolate in a microwavable bowl on Defrost (30%) for 2 minutes, stir, then cook for 2 minutes longer, continue in this way until chocolate is completely melted.
3. Beat egg yolks and 60 g/2 oz sugar until thick and creamy. Stir in melted chocolate and vanilla essence.
4. Beat egg whites until soft peaks form. Then gradually beat in remaining sugar and continue beating until stiff peaks form. Fold egg whites mixture, hazelnuts and breadcrumbs into chocolate mixture.
5. Spoon half the mixture into prepared muffin tray and cook, elevated, on Medium (50%) for 4 minutes. Cover and stand for 1 minute before turning out. Repeat with remaining mixture.
6. To make sauce, melt chocolate in a microwavable bowl as described in step 2. Stir in sugar and cool slightly. Add cream and liqueur and mix well to combine. Serve with puddings.

ingredients

- > **12 teaspoons lime marmalade, warmed**
- > **100 g/3 1/2 oz dark chocolate, broken into small pieces**
- > **4 eggs, separated**
- > **1/2 cup/100 g/3 1/2 oz caster sugar**
- > **1 teaspoon vanilla essence**
- > **100 g/3 1/2 oz hazelnuts, toasted and ground**
- > **1 cup/60 g/2 oz white breadcrumbs, made from stale bread**

chocolate fudge sauce

- > **100 g/3 1/2 oz dark chocolate, broken into small pieces**
- > **1 tablespoon caster sugar**
- > **1/2 cup/125 ml/4 fl oz cream**
- > **1 tablespoon orange-flavored liqueur**

....
Makes 12

tip from the chef

Take care when melting chocolate in the microwave as it holds its shape and can burn if overheated. Always stir before giving additional cooking time.

chocolate
and rum bread pudding

■□□ I Cooking time: 30 minutes - Preparation time: 10 minutes

method

1. Cut bread slices into 7.5 cm/3 in rounds using a pastry cutter, butter both sides. Place 2 bread rounds in the base of four individual 1¹/₂ cup/375 ml/12 fl oz capacity ovenproof dishes (a).
2. Combine eggs, sugar, milk, rum and 1 tablespoon cocoa powder (b) and beat until blended. Strain mixture over bread rounds.
3. Stand dishes in a baking dish. Pour in enough water to come halfway up sides of dishes. Sprinkle with remaining cocoa powder (c) and bake at 150°C/300°F/Gas 2 for 25-30 minutes or until firm.

ingredients

> **8 slices fruit loaf**
> **60 g/2 oz butter, softened**
> **4 eggs, lightly beaten**
> **2 tablespoons caster sugar**
> **2 cups/500 ml/16 fl oz milk**
> **1 tablespoon rum**
> **1¹/₂ tablespoons cocoa powder**

....
Serves 4

tip from the chef

An updated version of a traditional recipe that is sure to be a hit with family and friends.

a   b   c

chocolate
soufflé

■□□ I Cooking time: 25 minutes - Preparation time: 10 minutes

ingredients

> 1 1/2 **tablespoons butter**
> 1 1/2 **tablespoons flour**
> 1 1/4 **cups hot milk**
> 1/2 **teaspoon vanilla essence**
> 4 **tablespoons hot milk, extra**
> 100 g/3 1/2 **oz dark chocolate, melted**
> 4 **eggs, separated**
> 4 **tablespoons caster sugar**
> **icing sugar for dusting**

method

1. Melt butter in a medium saucepan over moderate heat, stir in flour and cook for 30 seconds. Remove from heat, stir in hot milk and vanilla essence, return to heat and slowly bring to the boil, stirring constantly until sauce thickens.
2. Mix extra milk into chocolate, add to sauce. Beat egg yolks, one at a time, into chocolate mixture, then beat in sugar.
3. Beat egg whites until soft peaks form. Fold into chocolate mixture, 1/2 cup at a time.
4. Grease four 3/4-cup capacity soufflé dishes and line the edge with a collar of greaseproof paper. Pour soufflé mixture into dishes, filling 3/4 way up.
5. Bake in moderate oven for 20-25 minutes. Remove greaseproof paper and dust top with icing sugar. Serve immediately.

....

Serves 4

tip from the chef
This delicate dessert results even more attractive if it is served with vanilla ice-cream or custard.

frozen
maple nut parfait

■ ■ □ | Cooking time: 0 minute - Preparation time: 10 minutes

method

1. Place sugar and water in a saucepan and heat over a low heat, stirring, until sugar dissolves. Bring to the boil and boil until syrup reaches soft ball stage or 118°C/244°F on a thermometer.

2. Place egg yolks in a bowl and beat until thick and pale. Gradually beat sugar syrup and maple syrup into egg yolks and continue beating until mixture cools.

3. Beat cream in a bowl until soft peaks form. Fold cream, macadamia nuts and chocolate into egg mixture.

4. Pour mixture into an aluminum foil-lined 15 x 25 cm/6 x 10 in loaf tin and freeze for 5 hours or until firm.

5. Turn parfait onto a serving plate, remove foil, cut into slices and drizzle with maple syrup.

ingredients

> 1 cup/220 g/7 oz caster sugar
> 1/2 cup/125 ml/4 fl oz water
> 6 egg yolks
> 1/2 cup/125 ml/4 fl oz maple syrup
> 600 ml/1 pt double cream
> 100 g/3 1/2 oz macadamia nuts, finely chopped
> 100 g/3 1/2 oz white chocolate, chopped
> extra maple syrup

....

Serves 8

tip from the chef

A garnish of fresh fruit and perhaps some almond-flavored biscotti are perfect partners for this light and luscious frozen dessert.

pink
and white mousse

■□□ | Cooking time: 0 minute - Preparation time: 15 minutes

ingredients

> **500 g/1 lb mixed berries of your choice**
> **1 cup/250 g/8 oz sugar**
> **1 tablespoon orange-flavored liqueur**
> **1/4 cup/60 ml/2 fl oz water**
> **6 egg yolks**
> **200 g/6 1/2 oz white chocolate, cut in pieces**
> **2 teaspoons vanilla essence**
> **1 2/3 cups/410 ml/13 fl oz double cream, whipped**
> **white chocolate shavings (page 60)**

tip from the chef
Garnish with additional fresh berries or red and white currants when available.

method

1. Place berries in a food processor or blender and process to make a purée. Press purée through a sieve into a saucepan (a). Stir in 1/3 cup/90 g/3 oz sugar and liqueur and bring to simmering over a low heat. Simmer, stirring occasionally, until mixture reduces to 1 cup/250 ml/8 fl oz. Remove pan from heat and set aside.

2. Place water, egg yolks and remaining sugar in a heatproof bowl set over a saucepan of simmering water and beat for 8 minutes or until mixture is light and creamy. Remove bowl from pan. Add chocolate (b) and vanilla essence and beat until mixture cools. Fold whipped cream into chocolate mixture. Divide mixture into two portions.

3. Stir berry purée into one portion of mixture (c) and leave one portion plain. Drop alternate spoonfuls of berry and plain mixtures into serving glasses (d). Using a skewer swirl mixtures to give a ripple effect. Refrigerate until firm. Just prior to serving decorate with chocolate shavings.

....
Serves 8

a

b

c

d

banana mousse

■□□ I Cooking time: 0 minute - Preparation time: 10 minutes

method

1. Place gelatin and boiling water in a bowl and stir until gelatin dissolves. Set aside to cool.
2. Place bananas, sugar and lemon juice in a food processor and process until smooth. Stir gelatin mixture into banana mixture.
3. Place cream and coconut milk in a bowl and beat until soft peaks form. Fold cream mixture into banana mixture.
4. Spoon mousse into six serving glasses. Divide melted chocolate between glasses and swirl with a skewer. Refrigerate for 2 hours or until set.

ingredients

> **1 tablespoon gelatin**
> **1/4 cup/60 ml/2 fl oz boiling water**
> **500 g/1 lb ripe bananas**
> **1/4 cup/60 g/2 oz sugar**
> **1 tablespoon lemon juice**
> **220 ml/7 fl oz double cream**
> **100 ml/3 1/2 fl oz coconut milk**
> **100 g/3 1/2 oz dark chocolate, melted**

....
Serves 6

tip from the chef

When available, dried banana chips make an attractive garnish with fresh mint leaves.

chocolate
mascarpone roulade

■□□ I Cooking time: 20 minutes - Preparation time: 10 minutes

ingredients
> **185 g/6 oz dark chocolate, broken into pieces**
> **$1/4$ cup/60 ml/2 fl oz strong black coffee**
> **5 eggs, separated**
> **$1/2$ cup/100 g/$3^1/2$ oz caster sugar**
> **2 tablespoons self-raising flour, sifted**
> **frosted rose petals**

mascarpone filling
> **375 g/12 oz mascarpone**
> **2 tablespoons icing sugar**
> **2 tablespoons brandy**
> **$1/2$ cup/125 g/4 oz chocolate hazelnut spread**

method
1. Place chocolate and coffee in a heatproof bowl set over a saucepan of simmering water and heat, stirring, until mixture is smooth. Cool slightly.
2. Beat egg yolks until thick and pale. Gradually beat in caster sugar. Fold chocolate mixture and flour into egg yolks.
3. Beat egg whites until stiff peaks form. Fold into chocolate mixture.
4. Pour mixture into a greased and lined 26 x 32 cm/ $10^1/2$ x $12^3/4$ in Swiss roll tin and bake at 160°C/325°F/Gas 3 for 20 minutes or until firm. Cool in tin.
5. To make filling, beat mascarpone, icing sugar and brandy in a bowl.
6. Turn roulade onto a clean tea-towel sprinkled with caster sugar. Spread with chocolate hazelnut spread and half the filling and roll up. Spread with remaining filling and decorate with frosted rose petals.

....
Serves 8-10

tip from the chef
To make frosted rose petals, lightly whisk egg white in a shallow bowl and dip in fresh, dry petals to lightly cover. Dip petals into caster sugar, shake off excess and stand on greaseproof paper to harden.

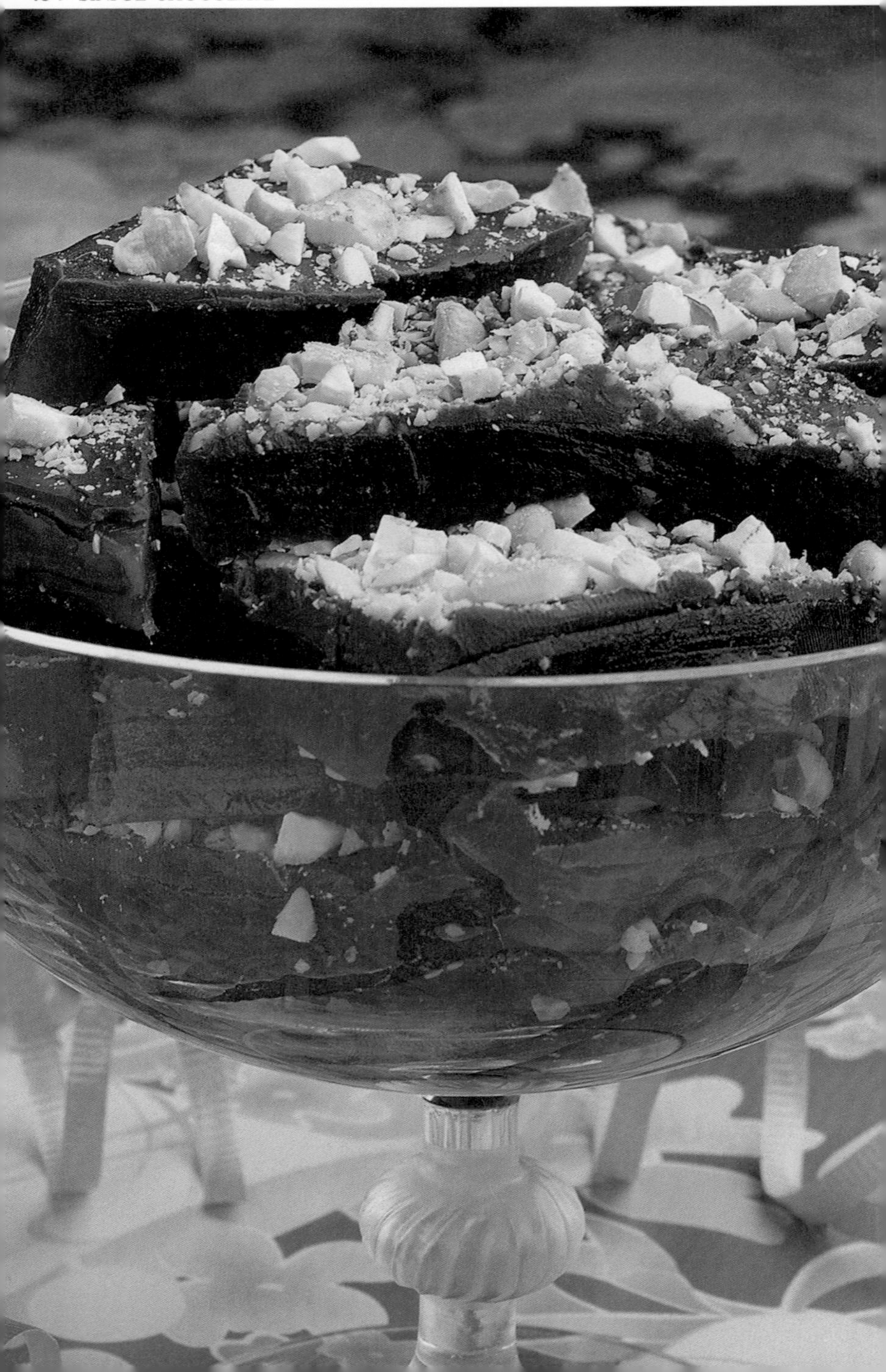

chocolate
cashew toffee

■□□ I Cooking time: 5 minutes - Preparation time: 10 minutes

method

1. Combine sugar, syrup, butter and vinegar in a saucepan, stir over heat, without boiling, until sugar is dissolved. Bring to the boil, cook, without stirring, until golden brown. Allow bubbles to subside.
2. Pour mixture into a greased shallow 19 x 29 cm/7½ x 11½ in baking dish, allow to set.
3. Melt chocolate and copha in a heatproof bowl set over a saucepan of simmering water, spread evenly over toffee. Sprinkle with cashews, allow to set.
4. Loosen toffee from pan with a knife, lift out onto a chopping board. Cut into chunks with a sharp knife. Store in a airtight container with greaseproof paper between layers.

ingredients

> **2 cups brown sugar, firmly packed**
> **½ cup light golden syrup**
> **185 g/6 oz butter**
> **2 tablespoons vinegar**
> **125 g/4 oz dark chocolate**
> **30 g/1 oz copha (vegetable shortening)**
> **125 g/4 oz roasted unsalted cashews, chopped**

....
Makes 60

tip from the chef

It is important to keep toffee in a dry place, otherwise it will get damp.

nuts truffles

■□□ I Cooking time: 0 minute - Preparation time: 15 minutes

ingredients

hazelnut truffles

> 200 g/6¹/2 oz white chocolate, broken into pieces
> 45 g/1¹/2 oz butter, chopped
> ¹/4 cup/60 ml/2 fl oz double cream
> 1 tablespoon hazelnut-flavored liqueur
> 125 g/4 oz hazelnuts, toasted, skins removed
> 60 g/2 oz desiccated coconut

almond truffles

> 185 g/6 oz milk chocolate, broken into pieces
> 90 g/3 oz butter, chopped
> ¹/2 cup/125 ml/4 fl oz double cream
> ¹/4 cup/60 ml/2 fl oz light golden syrup
> 1 tablespoon brandy
> 75 g/2¹/2 oz chopped dried figs
> 45 g/1¹/2 oz slivered almonds, toasted
> 60 g/2 oz flaked almonds, toasted

method

1. To make hazelnut truffles, place chocolate, butter, cream and liqueur in a heatproof bowl set over a saucepan of simmering water and heat, stirring (a), until mixture is smooth. Cool slightly. Stir until thick and pliable.

2. Roll tablespoons of mixture into balls (b). Press a hazelnut into the center of each ball and roll to enclose nut (c). Roll balls in coconut and refrigerate for 1 hour or until firm.

3. To make almond truffles, place chocolate, butter, cream, golden syrup and brandy in a heatproof bowl set over a saucepan of simmering water and heat, stirring, until mixture is smooth. Remove bowl from pan. Add figs and slivered almonds to chocolate mixture and mix well to combine. Chill mixture for 1 hour or until pliable.

4. Take tablespoons of mixture and roll into balls, then roll in flaked almonds. Place on nonstick baking paper and chill until required.

Makes 40 hazelnut truffles and 24 almond truffles

tip from the chef

You may also wish to toast the coconut used for rolling the hazelnut truffles, for a richer flavor.

If preferred, soft dried prunes or dates may be used in place of the figs for the almond truffles.

a   b   c

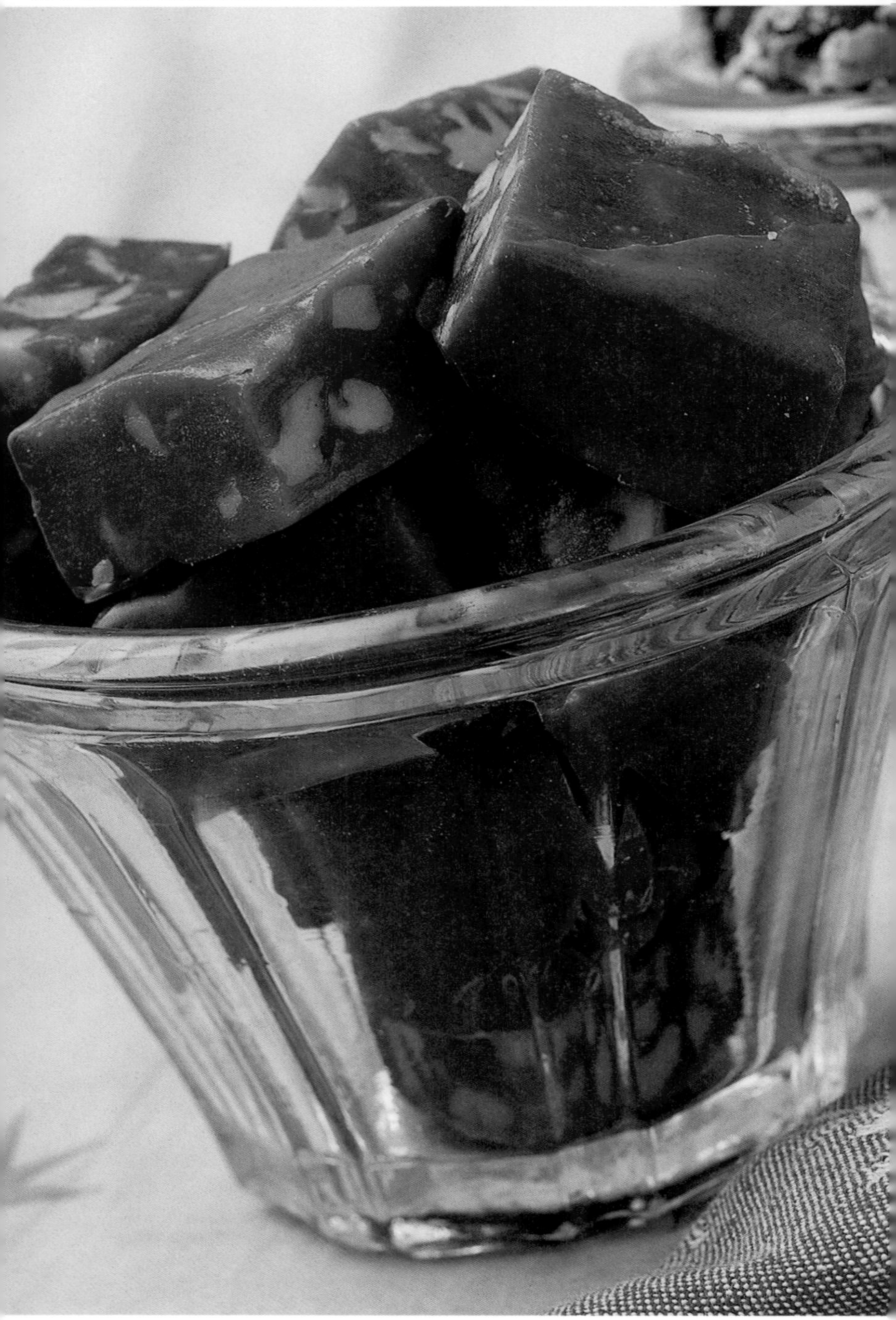

caramel
walnut petits fours

■□□ | Cooking time: 5 minutes - Preparation time: 10 minutes

method

1. Place caster sugar, brown sugar, cream, golden syrup and butter in a frying pan and heat over a low heat, stirring constantly, until sugar dissolves. As sugar crystals form on sides of pan, brush with a wet pastry brush.
2. Bring syrup to the boil and stir in bicarbonate of soda (a). Reduce heat and simmer until syrup reaches the hard ball stage or 120°C/250°F on a thermometer. Stir in walnuts (b) and vanilla essence.
3. Pour mixture into a greased and foil-lined 20 cm/8 in square cake tin. Set aside at room temperature for 5 hours or until caramel sets. Remove from tin and cut into 2 cm/3/4 in squares (c).
4. To make icing, combine chocolate and oil. Half dip caramels in melted chocolate, place on greaseproof paper and allow to set.

....
Makes 40

ingredients

> **1 cup/250 g/8 oz caster sugar**
> **1/2 cup/90 g/3 oz brown sugar**
> **2 cups/500 ml/16 fl oz double cream**
> **1 cup/250 ml/8 fl oz light golden syrup**
> **60 g/2 oz butter, chopped**
> **1/2 teaspoon bicarbonate of soda**
> **155 g/5 oz chopped walnuts**
> **1 tablespoon vanilla essence**

chocolate icing

> **375 g/12 oz dark or milk chocolate, melted**
> **2 teaspoons vegetable oil**

tip from the chef

For easy removal of caramel from the tin, allow the foil lining to overhang the tin on two opposite sides to form handles for lifting.

a

b

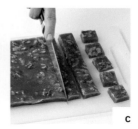
c

chocolate
nougat hearts

■□□ | Cooking time: 0 minute - Preparation time: 15 minutes

method

1. Place chocolate, butter and cream in a heatproof bowl set over a saucepan of simmering water and heat, stirring, until mixture is smooth.

2. Add nougat and almonds and mix well to combine. Pour mixture into a greased and lined 18 x 28 cm/7 x 11 in shallow cake tin. Refrigerate for 2 hours or until set.

3. Using a heart-shaped cutter, cut out hearts from set mixture.

ingredients

> **375 g/12 oz milk chocolate, broken into pieces**
> **45 g/1 1/2 oz butter, chopped**
> **1/2 cup/125 ml/4 fl oz double cream**
> **200 g/6 1/2 oz nougat, chopped**
> **100 g/3 1/2 oz almonds, toasted, chopped**

....

Makes 40

tip from the chef

Dip cutter into warm water and dry on a clean towel between each cut to achieve evenly straight edges.

chocolate panforte

■□□ I Cooking time: 30 minutes - Preparation time: 15 minutes

method

1. Place honey and sugar in a small saucepan and heat, stirring constantly, over a low heat until sugar dissolves. Bring to the boil, then reduce heat and simmer, stirring constantly, for 5 minutes or until mixture thickens.
2. Place almonds, hazelnuts, apricots, peaches, mixed peel, flour, cocoa powder and cinnamon in a bowl and mix to combine. Stir in honey syrup. Add chocolate and mix well to combine.
3. Line an 18 x 28 cm/7 x 11 in shallow cake tin with rice paper. Pour mixture into tin and bake at 200°C/400°F/Gas 6 for 20 minutes. Turn onto a wire rack to cool, then cut into small pieces.

....
Makes 32

ingredients

> 1 cup/250 ml/8 fl oz honey
> 1 cup/250 g/8 oz sugar
> 250 g/8 oz almonds, toasted, chopped
> 250 g/8 oz hazelnuts, toasted, chopped
> 125 g/4 oz glacé apricots, chopped
> 125 g/4 oz glacé peaches, chopped
> 100 g/3$^{1}/_{2}$ oz candied mixed peel
> 1$^{1}/_{2}$ cups/185 g/6 oz flour, sifted
> $^{1}/_{3}$ cup/45 g/1$^{1}/_{2}$ oz cocoa powder, sifted
> 2 teaspoons ground cinnamon
> 155 g/5 oz dark chocolate, melted
> rice paper

tip from the chef

If you don't have rice paper, cover the mold with greased greaseproof paper.

rosehip
pears with cocoa sauce

■□□ | Cooking time: 25 minutes - Preparation time: 10 minutes

ingredients

> **4 ripe, firm pears, peeled**
> **6 rosehip tea bags**

cocoa sauce
> **4 tablespoons butter**
> **1/4 cup brown sugar**
> **1/2 cup sour cream**
> **1/4 cup condensed milk**
> **4 tablespoons cocoa powder**
> **3 tablespoons water**

method

1. Place pears in a deep saucepan with water to cover, add tea bags and bring to simmering. Poach pears until tender, about 20 minutes.
2. To make sauce, melt butter in a medium saucepan over moderate heat. Add sugar, sour cream and condensed milk, stir constantly, do not boil.
3. Dissolve cocoa in water. Stir into sauce, bring to simmering and cook for 1 minute or until sauce thickens.
4. Pour a little sauce into the bottom of each serving glass and place a poached pear in the sauce. Garnish with mint if desired.

....

Serves 4

tip from the chef
The combination of pears and chocolate is delicious. If pears are not in season, you can use canned pears.

citrus pudding
with choc sauce

■☐☐ | Cooking time: 75 minutes - Preparation time: 15 minutes

method

1. Place butter and sugar in a bowl and beat until light and fluffy. Gradually beat in eggs. Add flour, milk, lemon curd and orange rind and mix well to combine.

2. Spoon mixture into a greased 4 cup/ 1 liter/1³/₄ pt capacity pudding basin. Cover with aluminum foil, then with basin lid. Place basin on a wire rack in a large saucepan with enough boiling water to come halfway up the side of the basin. Cover and boil for 1¹/₄ hours or until pudding is cooked when tested with a skewer, replacing water if necessary as pudding cooks.

3. To make sauce, place butter, chocolate, cream and rum in a heatproof bowl set over a saucepan of simmering water and heat, stirring, until mixture is smooth. Serve with pudding.

ingredients

> **90 g/3 oz butter, softened**
> **¹/₃ cup/75 g/2¹/₂ oz caster sugar**
> **2 eggs, lightly beaten**
> **1 cup/125 g/4 oz self-raising flour, sifted**
> **¹/₄ cup/60 ml/2 fl oz buttermilk or milk**
> **2 tablespoons lemon curd**
> **2 tablespoons finely grated orange rind**

rich chocolate sauce

> **60 g/2 oz butter**
> **200 g/6¹/₂ oz dark chocolate, broken into pieces**
> **1 cup/250 ml/8 fl oz double cream**
> **2 tablespoons rum**

....
Serves 6

tip from the chef
Slice pudding into wedges and pour sauce over pudding. Serve with a scoop of ice cream.

easy ideas

chocolate caraques

Spread a layer of melted chocolate over a marble, granite or ceramic work surface. Allow chocolate to set at room temperature. Then, holding a metal pastry scraper or a large knife at a 45° angle, slowly push it along the work surface away from you to form the chocolate into cylinders. If chocolate shavings form, then it is too cold and it is best to start again.

chocolate curls or shavings

To make curls, use chocolate at room temperature. To make shavings, chill the chocolate first. Using a vegetable peeler, shave the sides of the chocolate. Whether curls or shavings form depends on the temperature of the chocolate.

double chocolate strawberries

In separate heatproof bowls set over saucepans of simmering water melt 125 g/4 oz white chocolate and dark chocolate, along with 30 g/1 oz margarine each.
Hold large strawberries by the stem; dip 2/3 of each strawberry into white chocolate, hold to allow excess to run off. Place onto a foil covered tray, refrigerate until set.

Dip 1/3 of each strawberry into dark
chocolate, hold to allow excess to run off.
Place onto a foil covered tray, refrigerate
until set.

molded chocolates

solid chocolates

It is important to have the molds clean and dry. Fill the molds with melted chocolate and tap on a hard surface to remove air bubbles. Place molds in the freezer for 3 minutes or until set. When set remove from freezer and tap molds gently to remove chocolates.

filled chocolates

Quarter fill the molds with melted chocolate and tap to remove air bubbles. Brush chocolate evenly up the sides of the molds to make a shell and freeze 2 minutes or until set. Add a filling such as fondant, glacé fruit or liqueur. Fill the top with melted chocolate and tap to remove air bubbles. Return molds to the freezer for 3 minutes or until set. Remove from freezer and tap gently to remove. Larger chocolate cases to hold desserts can also be made in this way, using foil-lined individual metal flan tins, brioche or muffin pans as the molds. When set, remove from tins and fill with a dessert filling such as a mousse or a flavored cream.

marbled chocolates

Spoon a little melted white and dark chocolate separately into a dish. Using a teaspoon, swirl the white chocolate into the dark chocolate to make a marble pattern, then proceed as above.